The GREATEST POP HITS OF 2000

Project Manager: Carol Cuellar
Cover Design: Olivia D. Novak

CONTENTS

AMAZED

Words and Music by
MARV GREEN, AIMEE MAYO
and CHRIS LINDSEY

I wan-na spend the rest of my life_____ with you by my side____

_____ for-ev-er and ev-er.

Ev-'ry lit-tle thing that you do,_____ (Ev-'ry lit-tle thing that you do...)

Freely

N.C.

ev-'ry lit-tle thing that you do, ba-by, I'm a-mazed by____ you.

Verse 2:
The smell of your skin,
The taste of your kiss,
The way you whisper in the dark.
Your hair all around me,
Baby, you surround me;
You touch every place in my heart.
Oh, it feels like the first time every time.
I wanna spend the whole night in your eyes.
(To Chorus:)

AMERICAN PIE

Words and Music by
DON McLEAN

Slowly and freely ♩ = 72

Prologue:

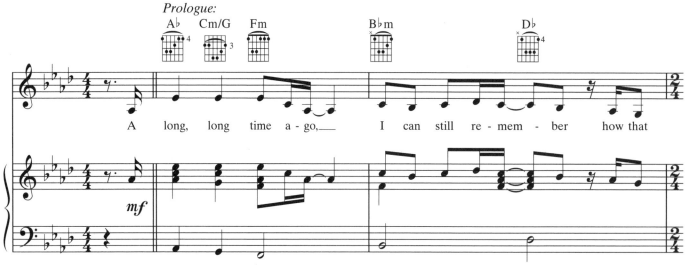

A long, long time a-go,___ I can still re-mem-ber how that

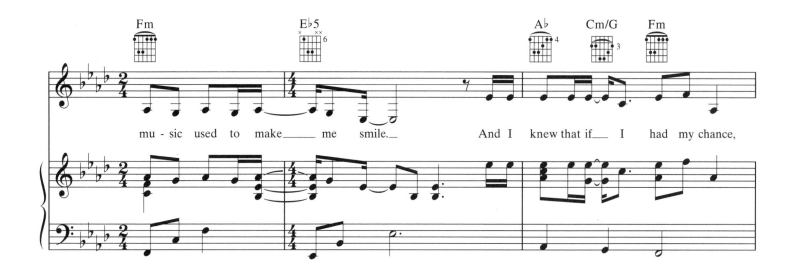

mu-sic used to make___ me smile.___ And I knew that if___ I had my chance,

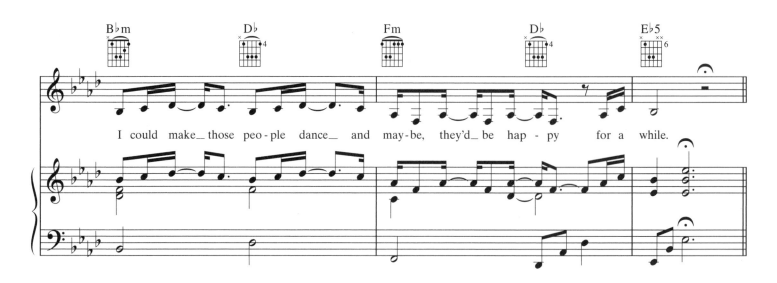

I could make___ those peo-ple dance___ and may-be, they'd___ be hap-py for a while.

American Pie - 7 - 1

Moderately fast ♩ = 124

E♭

Verse:
A♭

1. Did you___ write the
2. *See additional lyrics*

B♭m   D♭   B♭m

book of love?___ And do you___ have faith in God a - bove,___

Verse 2:
I met a girl who sang the blues
And I asked her for some happy news,
But she just smiled and turned away.
I went down to the sacred store,
Where I heard the music years before,
But the man there said the music wouldn't play.
And in the streets, the children screamed,
The lovers cried and the poets dreamed.
But not a word was spoken;
The church bells were all broken.
And the three men I admire most,
The Father, Son, and Holy Ghost,
They caught the last train for the coast
The day the music died.
And they were singin':
(To Chorus:)

BACK AT ONE

Words and Music by
BRIAN McKNIGHT

THE BEST DAY

Words and Music by
CARSON CHAMBERLAIN and DEAN DILLON

The Best Day - 4 - 1

Bridge:

1. A   A+   D   E

life."

2. A   Bm   A/C♯   D   Dmaj7

life."   Stand-in' in a lit-tle room,___ back of the church___

E   A   D   Dmaj9

___ with our tux - es on.   Look-in' at him,___ I say,___ "I can't be-

D.S.℅ al Coda

E

lieve, son, that you're___ grown."   He said,

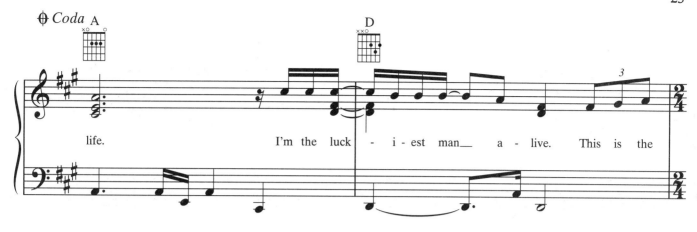

life. I'm the luck - i - est man___ a - live. This is the

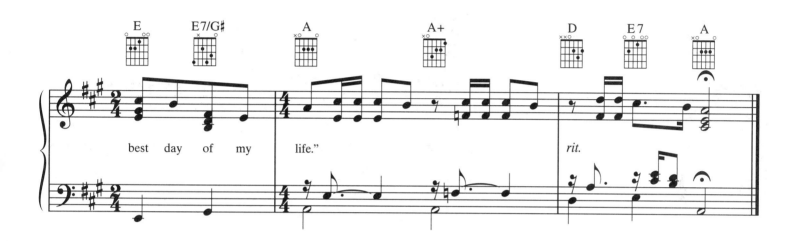

best day of my life." rit.

Verse 2:
His fifteenth birthday rolled around,
Classic cars were his thing.
When I pulled in the drive with that old Vette,
I thought the boy would go insane.
When you're in your teens, your dreams revolve
Around four spinnin' wheels.
We worked nights on end, 'til it was new again.
And as he sat behind the wheel, he said,
(To Chorus:)

Chorus 3:
"Dad, this could be the best day of my life.
I've been dreaming day and night of bein' like you.
Now it's me and her.
Watching you and Mom, I've learned
I'm the luckiest man alive
And this is the best day of my life."

BETTER OFF ALONE

Words and Music by
PRONTI and KALMANI

Better Off Alone - 5 - 1

Chorus:

Do you think you're bet - ter off___ a - lone?_____

Do you think you're bet - ter off___ a - lone?___

Do you think you're bet-

D.S. ℅ al Coda

ter off____ a - lone?_____

Coda

Talk to me.____

BREATHE

Words and Music by
HOLLY LAMAR and STEPHENIE BENTLEY

Breathe - 5 - 1

BYE BYE BYE

Words and Music by KRISTIAN LUNDIN,
JAKE and ANDREAS CARLSSON

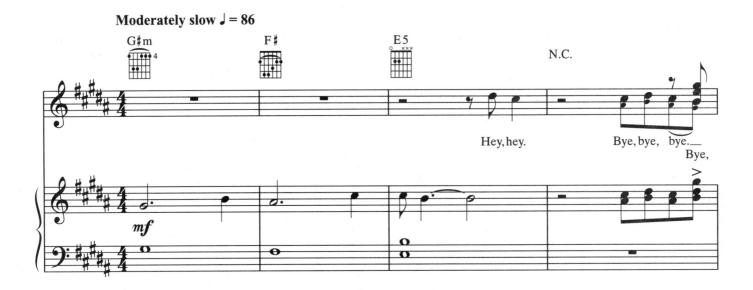

Verse:

Bye Bye Bye - 4 - 1

CAN'T TAKE THAT AWAY
(MARIAH'S THEME)

Words and Music by
DIANE WARREN and
MARIAH CAREY

Slowly ♩ = 52

Can't Take That Away (Mariah's Theme) - 6 - 1

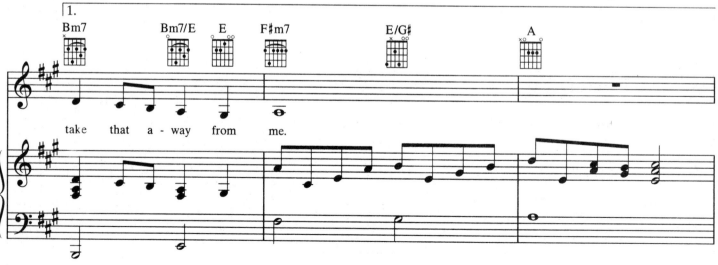

all. But I re- fuse to fal - ter in what I be - lieve or lose

Chorus:

faith in my dreams. 'Coz there's___ a___ light in me___ that shines___

To Coda

___ bright - ly._____ They can try,___ but they can't

1.

take that a - way from me.

42

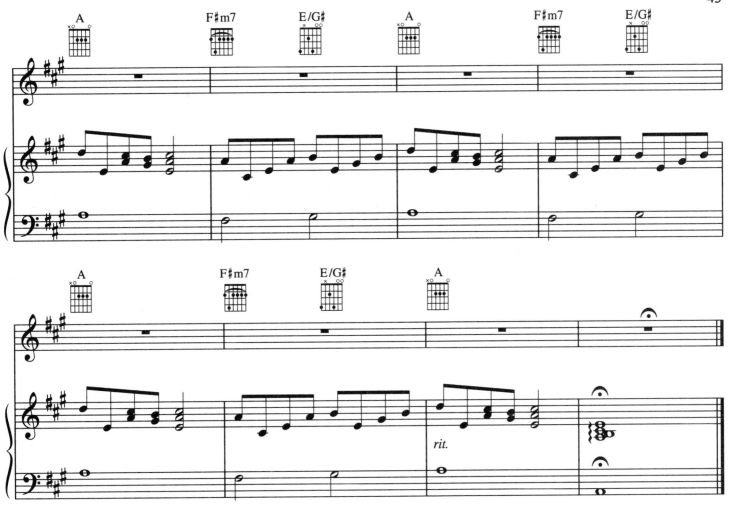

Verse 2:
They can do anything they want to you
If you let them in.
But they won't ever win
If you cling to your pride
And just push them aside.
See, I have learned there's an inner peace I own,
Something in my soul that they cannot possess.
So I won't be afraid and darkness will fade.
(To Chorus:)

Verse 3 (sung an octave higher):
They can say anything they want to say,
Try to break me down,
But I won't face the ground.
I will rise steadily,
Sailing out of their reach.
Oh, Lord, they do try hard to make me feel
That I don't matter at all.
But I refuse to falter in what I believe
Or lose faith in my dreams.
(To Chorus:)

CANDY

Words and Music by
DENISE RICH, DAVE KATZ
and DENNY KLEIMAN

Moderately ♩ = 100

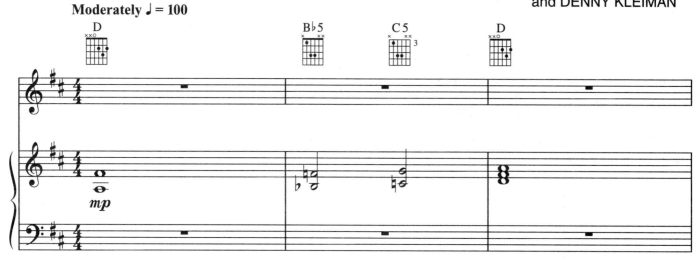

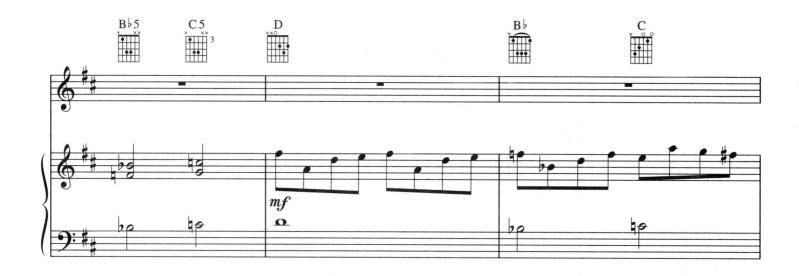

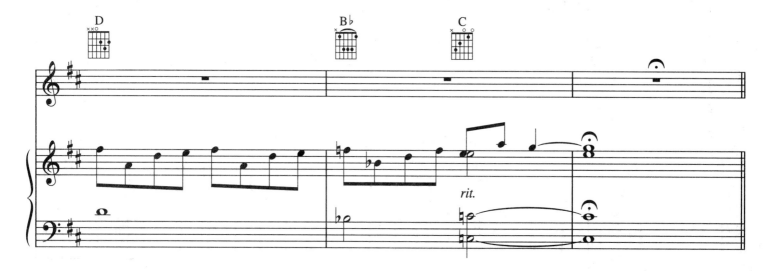

Candy - 6 - 1

Chorus:

come to me,__ ba-by, show me who you are.__ Sweet to me,__ like sug-

ar to my heart.__ I'm crav-ing for you. I'm miss-ing you__ like can-

dy, yeah, yeah.__ In-to you like can-dy. to you like can-dy.
So, ba-by,

come to me,__ ba-by, show me who you are.__ Sweet to me,__ like sug-

Chorus:

So, ba - by, come to me, ___ ba - by, show me who you are. ___

Sweet to me, ___ like sug - ar to my heart. ___ I'm crav - ing for you.

I'm miss - ing you ___ like can - dy, yeah, yeah. ___ So, ba - by,

I'm crav - ing for you. I'm miss - ing you ___ like can - dy, yeah, yeah. ___

COULD I HAVE THIS KISS FOREVER

Words and Music by
DIANE WARREN

Moderately slow ♩ = 82

Verse:

1. O - ver___ and o - ver,___ I look in___ your eyes. You are
2. O - ver___ and o - ver,___ I've dreamed of___ this night. Now you're

Could I Have This Kiss Forever - 6 - 1

S Chorus:

hold you for __ a life - time? Could I look in - to __ your eyes? __ Could I

have this night __ to share __ this night __ to - geth - er? Could I

hold you close __ be - side __ me? Could I hold you for __ all time? __ Could I, __

__ could I have this kiss __ for - ev - er? __ Could I, __

54

want all__ my days spent be - ing next to__ you, lived for__ just lov - ing__ you.

And, ba - by, oh by__ the way..._____ Could I

Coda N.C.

er?_____ Could I have this kiss__ for - ev - er?

Could I have this kiss__ for - ev - er?

D.S. % al Coda

Could I Have This Kiss Forever - 6 - 5

EVERYTHING YOU WANT

Tune Guitar down one half step

Words and Music by
MATT SCANNELL

1. Some-where there's speak-ing, it's al-read-y com-ing in. Oh,_ and it's ris-ing_ at the

2.3.4. *See additional lyrics*

Everything You Want - 5 - 1

And I don't know   why.   Why?

Repeat ad lib. and fade

Verse 2:
But under skinned knees and the skid marks,
Past the places where you used to learn,
You howl and listen,
Listen and wait for the
Echoes of angels who won't return.
(*To Chorus:*)

Verse 3:
You're waiting for someone
To put you together.
You're waiting for someone
To push you away.
There's always another wound to discover.
There's always something more you'd wish he'd say.
(*To Chorus:*)

Verse 4:
Out of the island,
Into the highway,
Past the places where you might have turned.
You never did notice,
But you still hide away
The anger of angels who won't return.
(*To Chorus:*)

EX-GIRLFRIEND

Words and Music by
GWEN STEFANI, TOM DUMONT
and TONY KANAL

Fast rock ♩ = 168

Ex-Girlfriend - 9 - 1

Verse 1:

Ex-Girlfriend - 9 - 2

Chorus:

Verse 3:

FALLS APART

Words and Music by
SUGAR RAY and DAVID KAHNE

Verses 1 & 2:

Verse 2:
You walk along by yourself.
There's no sound, nothing's changing.
They've gone away, left you there.
Emptiness, there's nothing you can share.
All those words that hurt you
More than you would let it show.
It comes apart by itself.
Always will and everything's wasted.
(To Chorus:)

FROM THE BOTTOM OF MY BROKEN HEART

Words and Music by
ERIC FOSTER WHITE

From the Bottom of My Broken Heart - 5 - 1

S: Chorus:

From the bot-tom of my bro-ken heart,____ there's just a thing____ or two I'd like you to know.____ You were my first____ love. You were my true____ love, from the first kiss-es to the ver-y last rose.____ From the

GIVE ME YOU

Words and Music by
DIANE WARREN

Give Me You - 5 - 1

prom-ise me that_ I'll have_ your heart._ You don't have to give the world to me,_ just

give me your word_ you will nev - er leave. 'Coz hav - ing you_ be - side_ me, I

have ev - 'ry - thing_ I need. Give_ me, give_ me you._

Chorus:

___ Give me you, give me all of you. Give_ me nights._ All my nights spent just hold-ing you. Give_ me days._

GET IT ON TONITE

Words and Music by JOERG EVERS,
JUERGEN KORDULETSCH, MONTELL JORDAN,
DARREN TODD BENBOW, ANTOINE B. WILSON,
BRIAN O. PALMER and SERGIO MOORE

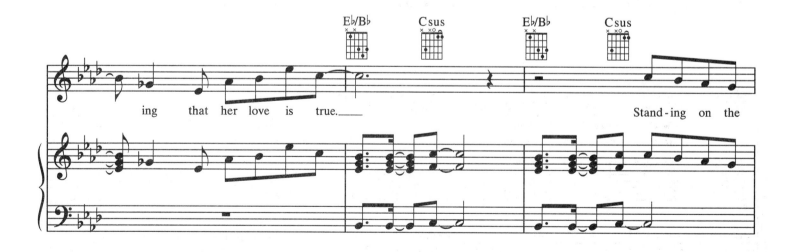

Verse 2:
Now she's lookin' at me,
But keep talkin'.
Oh, now she trying to ice you,
Let's start walking
Over on the dance floor.
It's her fault, but what can she do?
Tell me, baby.
If you're ready, (I'm ready.)
We can get it on. (We can get it on.)
I know where I went wrong.
(She's where you went wrong.)
With you is where I belong.
(To Bridge:)

GRADUATION
(Friends Forever)

Words and Music by
COLLEEN FITZPATRICK
and JOSH DEUTSCH

Slow shuffle ♩ = 80

Verse:

talked all night a-bout the rest of our lives,___ where we're gon-na be when we turn___ twen-ty - five.___

I keep think-ing times will nev - er change,___ keep on think-ing things will nev - er be the same. But when we

1. So we

Graduation - 7 - 1

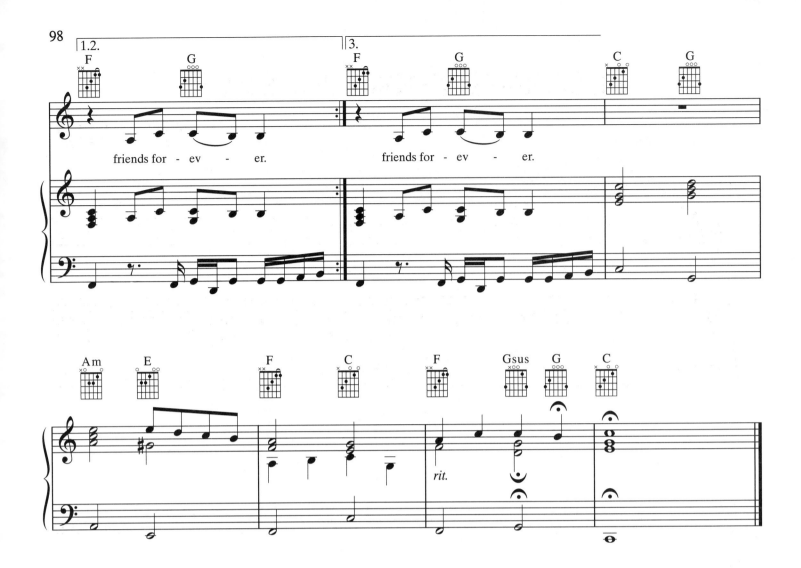

Verse 2:
So if we get the big jobs and we make the big money,
When we look back at now, will our jokes still be funny?
Will we still remember everything we learned in school,
Still be trying to break every single rule?
Will little brainy Bobby be the stockbroker man?
Can Heather find a job that won't interfere with her tan?
I keep, keep thinking that it's not goodbye,
Keep on thinking it's our time to fly.
And this is how it feels…
(To Chorus:)

Verse 3:
Will we think about tomorrow like we think about now?
Can we survive it out there, can we make it somehow?
I guess I thought that this would never end,
And suddenly it's like we're women and men.
Will the past be a shadow that will follow us around?
Will the memories fade when I leave this town?
I keep, keep thinking that it's not goodbye,
Keep thinking it's our time to fly.
(To Chorus:)

I LEARNED FROM THE BEST

Words and Music by
DIANE WARREN

From the Warner Bros. Motion Picture "ROMEO MUST DIE"

TRY AGAIN

Words and Music by
TIM MOSLEY and STEPHEN "STATIC" GARRETT

Try Again - 5 - 1

Chorus:

first you don't__ suc - ceed,_____ dust your-self off and try__

__ a - gain.__ You can dust it off and try__ a - gain,__ try a - gain. 'Cause if at

first you don't__ suc - ceed,_____ you can dust it off and try__

Repeat ad lib. and fade

__ a - gain.__ Dust your-self off and try__ a - gain,__ try a - gain. And if at

I WANT YOU TO NEED ME

Words and Music by
DIANE WARREN

I Want You to Need Me - 5 - 1

Chorus:

Lyrics:

I wan-na be your fan-ta-sy,___ and be your re-al-i-ty,___ and ev-

I wan-na be your deep-est kiss,___ the an-swer to your ev-'ry wish,___ and all___

'ry-thing___ be-tween.___ } I want you to need___ me___ like the

you ev-er need.___ }

air you___ breathe.___ I want you to feel___ me___ in

ev-'ry-thing.___ I want you to see___ me___ in your

ev-'ry__ dream,__ I want you to taste____ me, feel me, breathe me, need me.__ I want you to need__

__ me, need_ me like I need you.   need me.__ I want you to need____ me, need_ me.   'Coz

Bridge:

I   need_ you____   more than you_ could know.____   And

I   need_ you____   to nev-er, nev-er let__ me go.____   And

114

I Want You to Need Me - 5 - 4

I WAS BORN TO LOVE YOU

Words and Music by
ERIC CARMEN and
ANDY GOLDMARK

Verse 1:

1. I nev-er real-ly un-der-stood_ love,__ no, not un-til I saw your_ face, then I

knew what I'd been miss-ing for all___ my___ life.

I Was Born to Love You - 4 - 1

Verses 2 & 3:

2. I nev-er let my-self be-lieve__ it, no, not till I looked in your_ eyes, then I
3. There's no need to ev-er doubt_ it. You set my love free when you_ o-pened the

knew I found all I__ need the mo-ment that I found_ you.
door. You changed ev-'ry-thing. You're all that I'm liv-ing___ for. } I was born_

Chorus:

__ to love_ you, born__ to be right_ here by__ your side,_

__ through all your dark-est nights._ I was born__ to love_ you.__

I Was Born to Love You - 4 - 2

IF I DIDN'T LOVE YOU

Words and Music by
JUNIOR MILES and
BRUCE ROBERTS

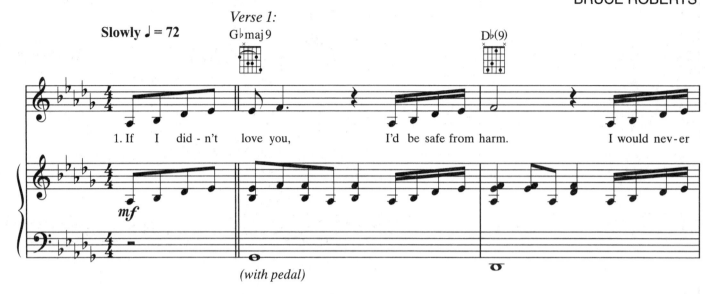

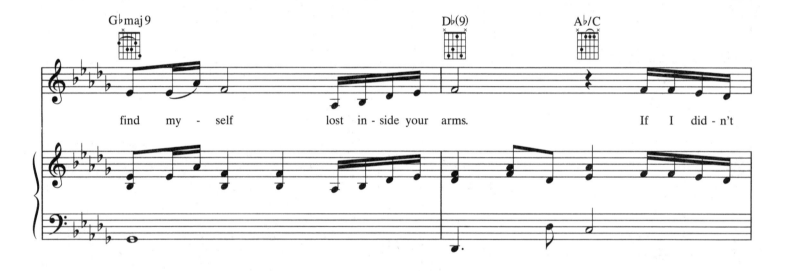

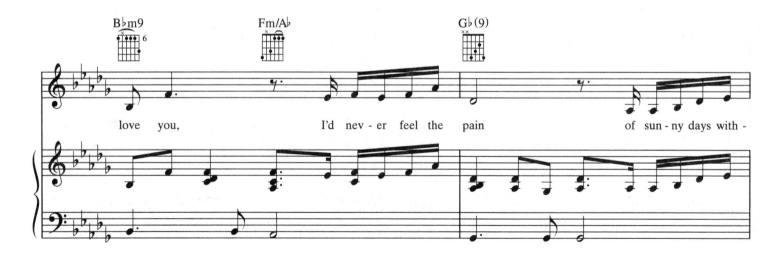

If I Didn't Love You - 6 - 1

Chorus 2:

How can there be___ mu - sic___ in the

way you___ touch? I can't be - lieve that some - how I be -

lieve in you so much. Now, you've come and taught___ me___ how to

give you my heart,___ and make me feel at last, that the

IT DON'T MATTER TO THE SUN

Words and Music by
GORDON KENNEDY, WAYNE KIRKPATRICK
and TOMMY SIMS

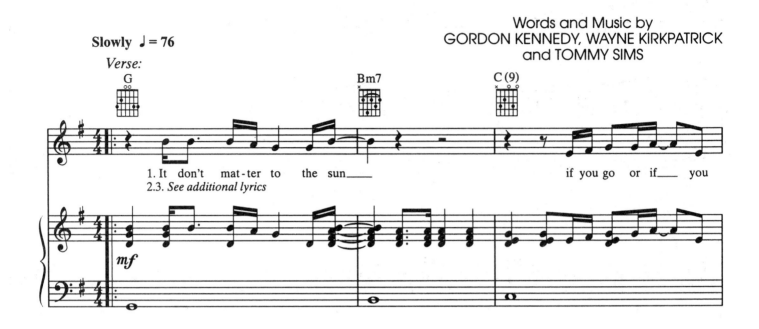

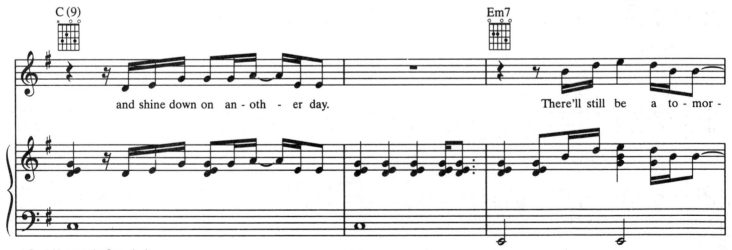

It Don't Matter to the Sun - 4 - 1

Verse 2:
It ain't gonna stop the world
If you walk out that door.
This old world will just keep on turnin' 'round
Like it did the day before.
You see, to them it makes no difference.
They'll just keep on keepin' time.
'Cause it ain't gonna stop the world out there,
But it'll be the end of mine.
(To Chorus:)

Verse 3:
It don't matter to the moon
If you're not in my life.
I know the moon will just keep hangin' 'round
Like it's just another night.
He'll find another place to shine down
On some other lover's dream.
'Cause it don't matter to the moon, no, babe,
But it sure do matter to me.

IT'S GONNA BE ME

Words and Music by
MAX MARTIN, RAMI
and ANDREAS CARLSSON

Moderately slow ♩ = 82

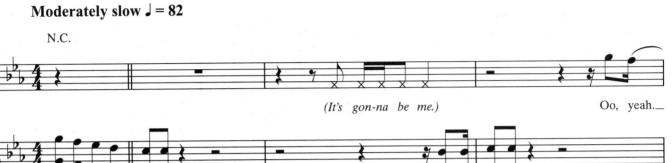

(It's gon-na be me.)   Oo, yeah._

Verse:

1. You might've been hurt, babe, that ain't no lie._
2. *See additional lyrics*

You've seen them all come and__ go,__ oh.__

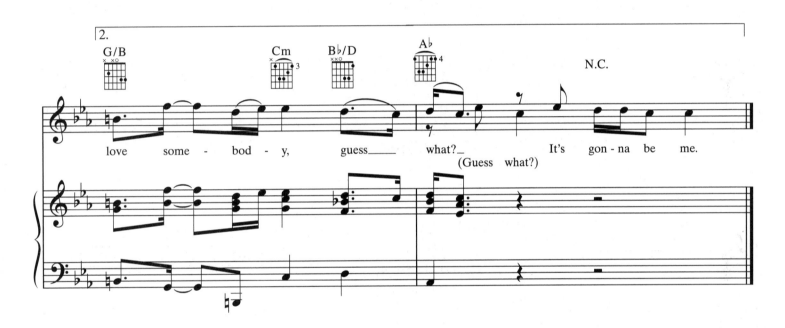

Verse 2:
You've got no choice, babe,
But to move on, you know
There ain't no time to waste,
 'Cause you're just too blind to see.
But in the end you know it's gonna be me.
You can't deny,
So just tell me why…
(To Chorus:)

KRYPTONITE

Words and Music by
MATT ROBERTS, BRAD ARNOLD
and TODD HARRELL

Kryptonite - 6 - 1

Verse 1:

1. Well, I took a walk around the world to ease my troubled mind. I left my body laying

some-where in the sands of time. And I watched the world float to the dark side of the moon.

And I feel there's nothing I can do. Yeah.

Verses 2 & 3:

2. I watched the world___ float to the dark side of the moon.___ Af-ter all I knew, it had to

3. *See additional lyrics*

be some-thing to do with you. I real-ly don't mind what hap-pens now and then, as

long as you'll be___ my friend___ in the end.___ If I go cra-zy, then will

you still call me su-per-man?___ If I'm a-live and well, will you be there___ hold-ing my hand?_

I'll keep you by my side with my su-per-hu - man might.___ Kryp - to - nite.___

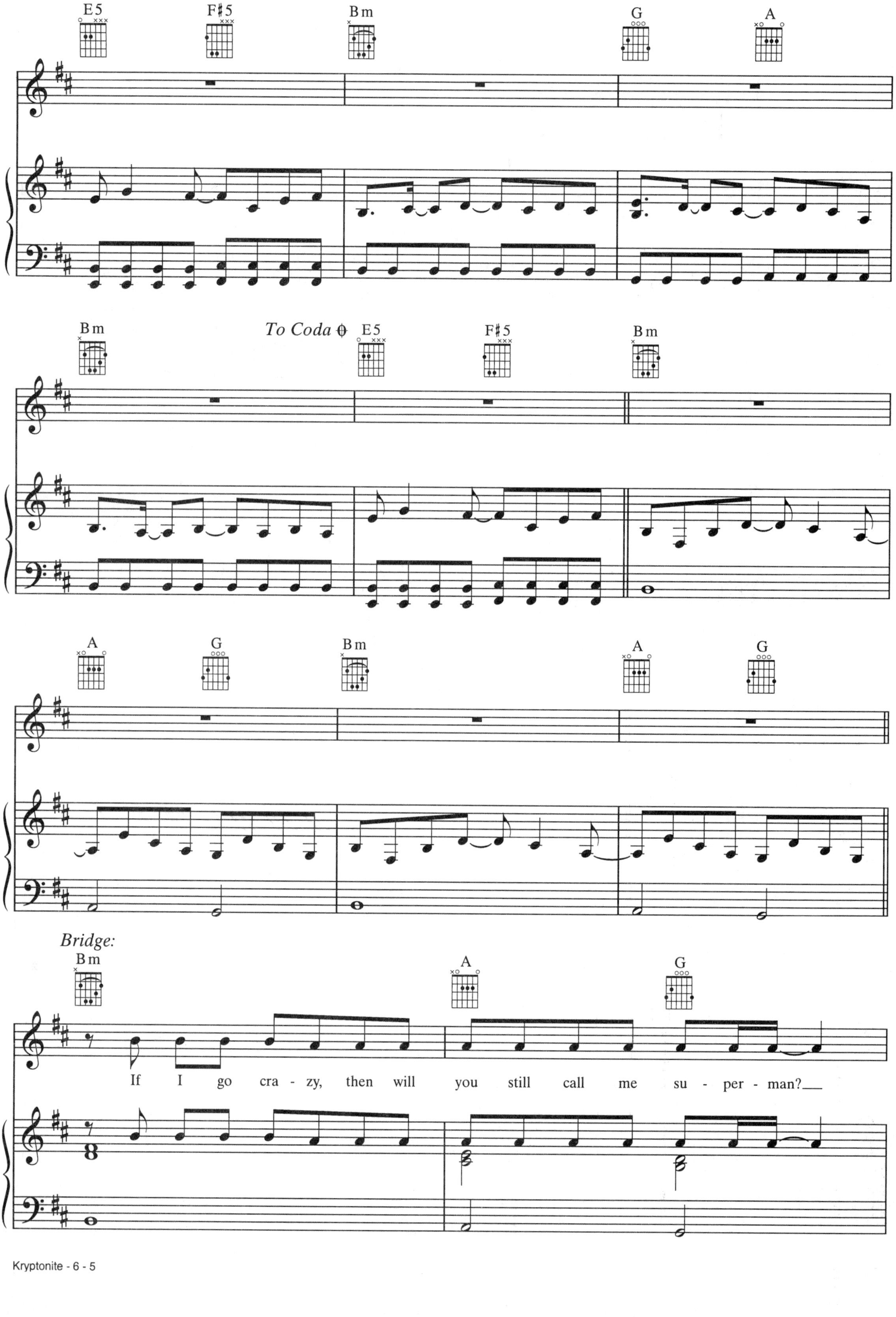

E5
F♯5
Bm
G
A
Bm
To Coda ⊕
E5
F♯5
Bm
A
G
Bm
A
G
Bridge:
Bm
A
G
If I go cra - zy, then will you still call me su - per - man?

D.S. % al Coda

⊕ Coda

Verse 3:
You called me strong, you called me weak,
But still your secrets I will keep.
You took for granted all the times I never let you down.
You stumbled in and bumped your head,
If not for me, then you would be dead.
I picked you up and put you back on solid ground.
(To Chorus:)

THE MAGIC OF LOVE

Lyrics by
ALAN and MARILYN BERGMAN

Music by
LIONEL RICHIE

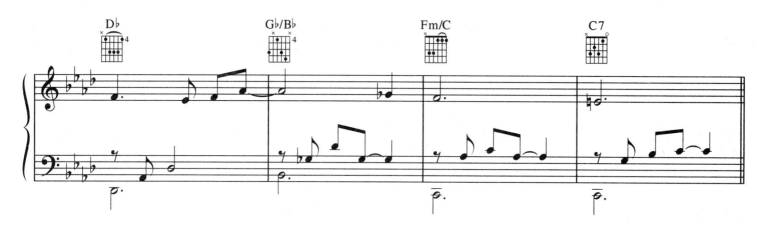

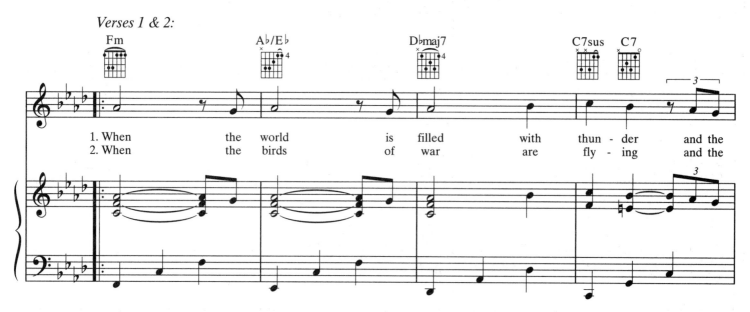

*Play chords 2nd time only.

Chorus:

But there's some - thing in - side us that

looks to the sun.

We dream that this light will guide us with

love for ev - 'ry - one.

MARIA MARIA

Words and Music by
WYCLEF JEAN, JERRY DUPLESSIS, CARLOS SANTANA,
KARL PERAZZO and RAUL REKOW

Moderately ♩ = 98

Intro:
N.C.

La - dies___ and gents,___ turn up___ your sound___ sys - tem___ to the

sound of Car - los San - ta - na and the G and B Pro - duct.

Ghet - to___ blues___ from the ref - u - gee___ camp.

Oh, Ma - ri - a, Ma - ri -

Maria Maria - 7 - 1

Bridge:

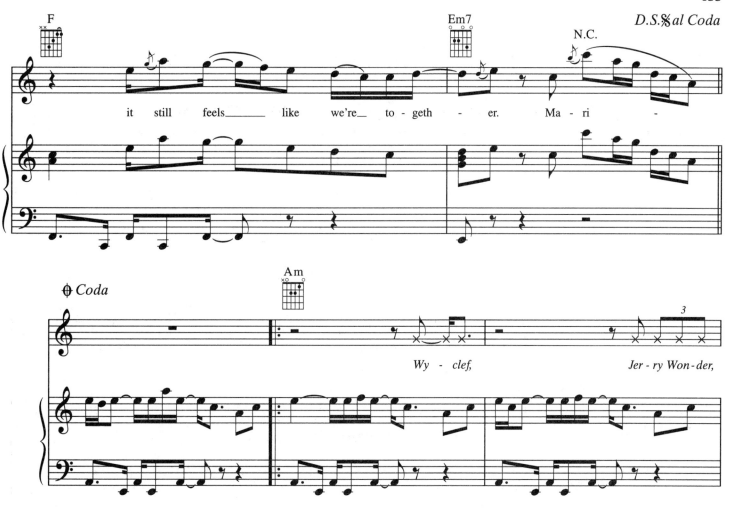

it still feels___ like we're___ to-geth - er. Ma - ri -

Wy - clef,

Jer - ry Won-der,

Mis - ter___ San - ta - na,

G and B.

Repeat ad lib. and fade

Verse 2:
I said, "A la favella los colores."
The streets are getting hotter.
There is no water
To put out the fire.
Mi canto, la esperanza.
Se mira Maria on the corner
Thinking of ways to make it better.
Then I looked up in the sky
Hoping the days of paradise.

NO MORE RAIN
(IN THIS CLOUD)

Words and Music by
ANGIE STONE, JAMES WEATHERLY
and GORDON CHAMBERS

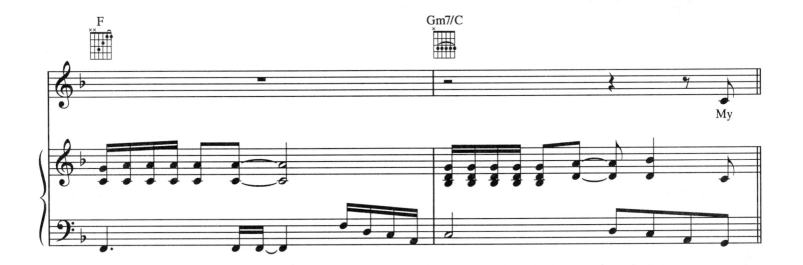

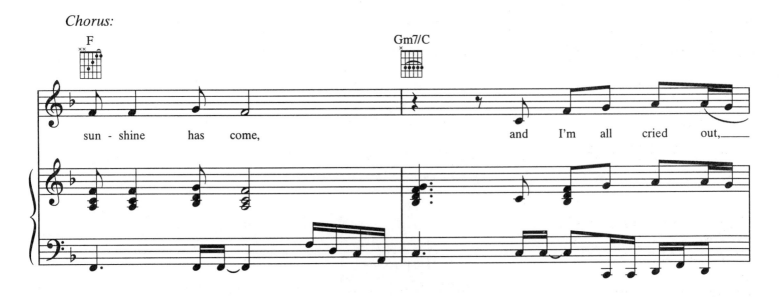

No More Rain (In This Cloud) - 7 - 1

Verse 1:

smile you used to wear___ seems a lit-tle bit out of place? Just

hold,_____ hold on,___ in

time,_____ it gets a lit-tle bet-ter. My

Chorus:

sun - shine has come, and I'm all cried out,___

F

Gm7/C

and there's no more rain_____ in this cloud.___ My

F

Gm7/C

sun - shine has come, and I'm all cried out,_____

F

Gm7/C

Repeat ad lib. and fade

and there's no more rain_____ in this cloud.___ My

Verse 3:
So, you want to live,
Then, to you I shall give
All the space that you requested.
Hope you don't live to regret it.
So, you say you're in your prime.
Baby, don't waste your time.
Remember my love.
It's only a thin line.
(Between love, between hate.)
(To Chorus:)

OOPS!... I DID IT AGAIN

Words and Music by
MAX MARTIN and RAMI

Moderately ♩ = 94

Oops!... I Did It Again - 7 - 1

THE ONE

Words and Music by
MAX MARTIN and BRIAN T. LITTRELL

PRIVATE EMOTION

Words and Music by
ROB HYMAN and ERIC BAZILIAN

Private Emotion - 5 - 1

Verse 2:
When your soul is tired
And your heart is weak,
Do you think of love
As a one-way street?
Well, it runs both ways.
Open up your eyes,
Can't you see me here?
How can you deny?
(To Chorus:)

Verse 3:
Every endless night
Has a dawning day.
Every darkest sky
Has a shining ray.
It takes a lot to laugh
As your tears go by.
But you can find me here
Till your tears run dry.
(To Chorus:)

SHOW ME THE MEANING OF BEING LONELY

Words and Music by
MAX MARTIN and HERBERT CRICHLOW

182

184

Chorus:

SMOOTH

Lyrics by
ROB THOMAS

Music by
ITAAL SHUR and ROB THOMAS

Moderately ♩ = 114

Verse:

1. Man, it's a hot one,

2. *See additional lyrics*

like sev-en in-ches from the mid-day sun.___ Well, I hear you whis-per and the

Smooth - 5 - 4

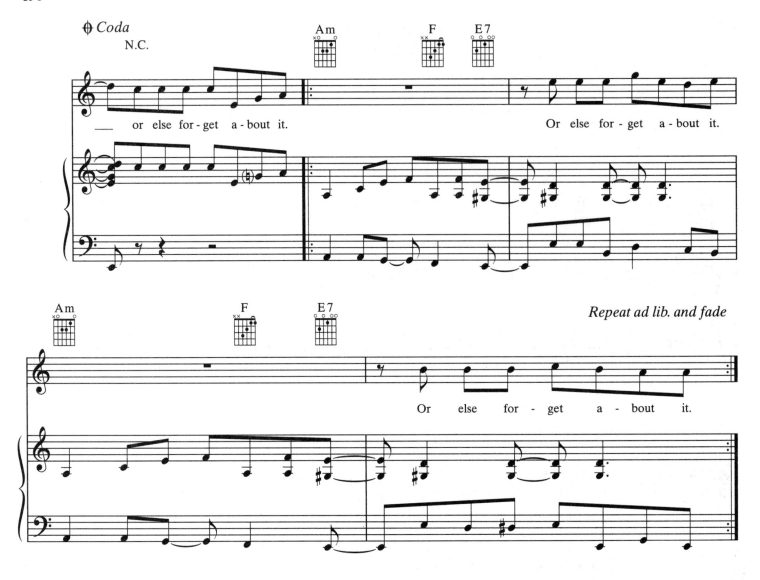

Verse 2:
Well, I'll tell you one thing,
If you would leave, it be a crying shame.
In every breath and every word
I hear your name calling me out, yeah.
Well, out from the barrio,
You hear my rhythm on your radio.
You feel the tugging of the world,
So soft and slow, turning you 'round and 'round.
(To Pre-Chorus:)

From the Motion Picture DOGMA

STILL

Tune Guitar:
⑥ = D ③ = G
⑤ = A ② = B
④ = D ① = D

Words and Music by
ALANIS MORISSETTE

Slowly ♩ = 74

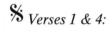

1. I am the harm that you in - flict.
4. I am your trag - e - dy and your for-tune.

I am your bril - liance and your frus - tra - tion.
I am your cri - sis and your de - light.

*Original recording in D♭.

Still - 7 - 1

I am your char-i-ty and your___ rape.
I am your yearn-ing and your___ sweat.
I am your sick-ness and con-va-les-cence.

I am your grasp-ing and ex-pec-ta-tion.
I am your faith-less and your re-li-gion.
I am your weap-ons and your light.

I see you___
I see you___
I see you___

Chorus:

a-vert-ing your glanc-es.___ I see you___
al-ter-ing his-to-ry.___ I see you___
hold-ing your grudg-es.___ I see you___

cheer-ing on a war.___ I see you___
a-bus-ing the land.___ I see you___
gun-ning them down.___ I see you___

Repeat ad lib. and fade

*First time only.

STOP (ASÍ)

Spanish Lyrics by
ANGIE CHIRINO, EMILIO ESTEFAN, JR.
and JON SECADA

Words and Music by
EMILIO ESTEFAN, JR., JON SECADA,
GEORGE NORIEGA and TIM MITCHELL

Stop (Así) - 6 - 1

Verse:

1. I wan-na take___ you to___ an-oth-er place___ and time___ so
1. Quie-ro lle-var-te_has-ta___ la ci-ma del___ pla-cer___
2. *See additional lyrics*

I can feel___ you move___ and breathe_ all o-ver me_ in-side.
y sen-tir___ tu_a-lien-to na-ve-gar so-bre___ mi piel.

Don't be a-fraid_ to tell___ me how___ you want_ to feel.___ Just
Yo so-lo pien-so en___ la po-si-bi-li-dad.___ Oo,

tell_ me what you want,___ and ba-by, I___ will make_ it real.___
di-me___ co-mo_ha-cer, tu sue-ño re-al-i-dad.

Stop (Así) - 6 - 2

Verse 2:
Look into my eyes and tell me what you wanna see.
I promise I will make your wish come true if you believe.
When I look at you, I know exactly what I need.
If you tell me what you want, I'll show you what I got in me.
(To Chorus:)

Verso 2:
Mírame a los ojos,
Dime lo que quieras ver.
Todos tus deseos te prometo complacer.
Sé que necesito tus encantos probar.
Sólo pide mi amor, todo te lo voy a dar.
(A Coro:)

SWEAR IT AGAIN

Words and Music by
WAYNE HECTOR and STEVE MAC

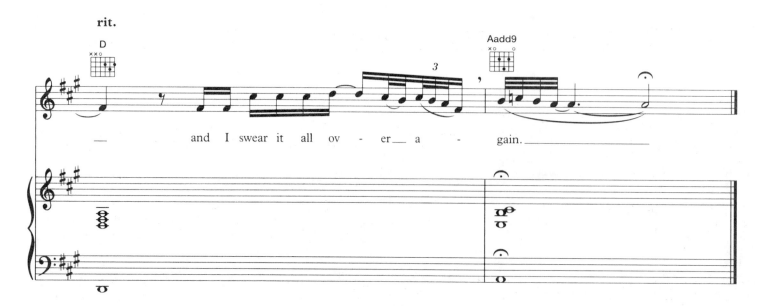

BE WITH YOU

Words and Music by
ENRIQUE IGLESIAS,
PAUL BARRY and MARK TAYLOR

Mon-day night and I feel so low.__ Count the hours but they go so slow.__

be with you. __

I can't sleep, I'm up all night. __ Through these tears I

try to __ smile. __ I know the touch of your hand can

THAT'S THE WAY IT IS

Words and Music by
MAX MARTIN, KRISTIAN LUNDIN
and ANDREAS CARLSSON

Verse:

read your mind and I know your story, I
ques-tion me for a sim-ple an-swer,

That's the Way It Is - 6 - 1

Chorus:

I TURN TO YOU

Words and Music by
DIANE WARREN

I Turn to You - 6 - 1

Chorus:

from the storm,___ for a friend,___ for a love___ to keep___ me safe___

___ and warm,___ I turn to you._____ For the strength___

to be strong,___ for the will___ to cary on,___ for

ev - 'ry - thing___ you do,___ for ev - 'ry - thing___ that's true,___ I turn to you.___

UNTITLED
(HOW DOES IT FEEL)

Words and Music by
D'ANGELO and RAPHAEL SAADIQ

Repeat ad lib. and fade

Verse 2:
I wanna stop silly little games
U and me play.
And I am feeling right on
If u feel the same way, baby.
Let me know right away.
I'd love to make u wet
In between your thighs, 'cause
I love when it comes inside u.
I get so excited when I am around u.
(To Chorus:)

WHAT A GIRL WANTS

Words and Music by
GUY ROCHE and
SHELLY PEIKEN

Slow, funky groove ♩ = 72

Chorus:

What a girl wants, what a girl needs, what-ev-er makes__ me hap-py sets__

__ you free. What a girl wants, what a girl needs, what-ev-er keeps__ me in__ your arms.__

F#m7   A9   Dmaj9   G7

1. I wan-na

What a Girl Wants - 8 - 1

Verse 2:
A weaker man might have walked away, but you had faith,
Strong enough to move over and give me space
While I got it together,
While I figured it out.
They say if you love something, let it go;
If it comes back, it's yours.
That's how you know it's for keeps, yeah, it's for sure,
And you're ready and willin' to give me more than…
(To Chorus:)

WE CAN'T BE FRIENDS

Words and Music by
SHEP CRAWFORD and JIMMY RUSSELL

He: 1. To just act_ like_ we nev-er_ were,_ to come a-round_ and not show_____ her._____ How dare we_ greet_____ by shak-ing_ hands,_ just

242

246

We Can't Be Friends - 7 - 7

I WILL LOVE AGAIN

Words and Music by
PAUL BARRY and MARK TAYLOR

Moderately fast ♩ = 128

Verse:

1. Did I ev-er tell you how you live_
2. Peo-ple nev-er tell you the way they real-

_ in me
ly feel.

ev-'ry wak-ing mo-ment,
I would die for you_ glad-ly if I

e-ven in_ my dreams?_
knew it was_ for real._

And if all this talk_ is cra-
So if all this talk_ sounds cra-

I Will Love Again - 5 - 1

Heav - en on - ly knows_____ I will love a -
gain.____ I will love a - gain.
I will love a - gain.____
One day,__ I know.

2 etc. vocal ad lib.

Repeat ad lib. and fade

TEN YEARS OF MUSIC HISTORY
REMEMBERING THE '90s SERIES

This series is an anthology of music from 1990-2000. Each volume includes artists' works and biographies!

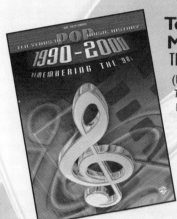

Ten Years of Pop Music History
The Red Book

(MFM0004)

Titles include: All for Love • Always Be My Baby • ...Baby One More Time • Believe • Coming Out of the Dark • Foolish Games • Here I Am (Come and Take Me) • How 'Bout Us • I Don't Want to Miss a Thing • Just Another Day • (God Must Have Spent) A Little More Time on You • More Than Words • Music of My Heart • Show Me the Way • Smooth • Something to Talk About • That's the Way It Is • Un-Break My Heart • You Were Meant for Me and many more.

Ten Years of Pop Music History
The Blue Book

(MFM0005)

Titles include: Back at One • Because You Loved Me • Breakfast at Tiffany's • Change the World • Constant Craving • Don't Cry for Me Argentina • Dreaming of You • From a Distance • Genie in a Bottle • I Do (Cherish You) • I Will Always Love You • If It Makes You Happy • Ironic • Killing Me Softly • Larger Than Life • Love Is All Around • Love Will Keep Us Alive • One of Us • Sunny Came Home and many more.

Ten Years of Country Music History
The Orange Book

(MFM0006)

Titles include: Angels Among Us • Any Man of Mine • A Bad Goodbye • Don't Take the Girl • Forever's As Far As I'll Go • From Here to Eternity • Go Away, No Wait a Minute • I Can Love You Like That • I Cross My Heart • I Do (Cherish You) • I Swear • I'd Like to Have That One Back • If Tomorrow Never Comes • The River • This Kiss • A Thousand Miles from Nowhere • Unanswered Prayers • When You Say Nothing at All • You Light Up My Life and many more.

Ten Years of Country Music History
The Green Book

(MFM0007)

Titles include: Amazed • Breathe • Commitment • The Dance • From This Moment On • How Do I Live • In Another's Eyes • My Maria • Please Remember Me • Pocket of a Clown • Put Yourself in My Shoes • Something in Red • Standing Outside the Fire • Strawberry Wine • There's Your Trouble • 26¢ • Two Sparrows in a Hurricane • What Might Have Been • Years From Here and many more.

Ten Years of Movie Music History
The Yellow Book

(MFM0009)

Titles include: Against the Wind (from *Forest Gump*) • At the Beginning (from *Anastasia*) • Don't Cry for Me Argentina (from *Evita*) • I Believe I Can Fly (from *Space Jam*) • I Say a Little Prayer (from *My Best Friend's Wedding*) • Music of My Heart (from *Music of the Heart*) • The Prayer (from *Quest for Camelot*) • Take Me to the River (from *The Commitments*) • Theme from *Jurassic Park* • There's Something About Mary (from *There's Something About Mary*) and many more.

Ten Years of Movie Music History
The Purple Book

(MFM0010)

Titles include: Anyone at All (from *You've Got Mail*) • Colors of the Wind (from *Pocahontas*) • Duel of the Fates (from *Star Wars: Episode I The Phantom Menace*) • I Will Remember You (from *The Brothers McMullen*) • Kissing You (Love Theme from *Romeo + Juliet*) • Once in a Lifetime (from *Only You*) • Something to Talk About (from *Something to Talk About*) • That Thing You Do (from *That Thing You Do!*) • Uninvited (from *City of Angels*) and many more.